# TAG THIS!

## A DOODLE BOOK

PSS!
PRICE STERN SLOAN
An Imprint of Penguin Group (USA) Inc.

PRICE STERN SLOAN
Published by the Penguin Group
Penguin Group (USA) Inc., 375 Hudson Street, New York, New York 10014, USA
Penguin Group (Canada), 90 Eglinton Avenue East, Suite 700,
Toronto, Ontario M4P 2Y3, Canada
(a division of Pearson Penguin Canada Inc.)
Penguin Books Ltd., 80 Strand, London WC2R 0RL, England
Penguin Group Ireland, 25 St. Stephen's Green, Dublin 2, Ireland
(a division of Penguin Books Ltd.)
Penguin Group (Australia), 250 Camberwell Road, Camberwell, Victoria 3124, Australia
(a division of Pearson Australia Group Pty. Ltd.)
Penguin Books India Pvt. Ltd., 11 Community Centre,
Panchsheel Park, New Delhi—110 017, India
Penguin Group (NZ), 67 Apollo Drive, Rosedale, Auckland 0632, New Zealand
(a division of Pearson New Zealand Ltd.)
Penguin Books (South Africa) (Pty.) Ltd., 24 Sturdee Avenue,
Rosebank, Johannesburg 2196, South Africa

Penguin Books Ltd., Registered Offices: 80 Strand, London WC2R 0RL, England

Photo credits: pages 4–5, 118–119: © Nicholas Belton/iStockphoto; pages 6–7: © Nate Strandberg/iStockphoto;
pages 8–9: © Nicholas Monu/iStockphoto; pages 10–11: © Sascha Burkard/iStockphoto; pages 12–13:
© Özgür Donmaz/iStockphoto; pages 14–15, 36–37, 98–99: © Joe Potato Photo/iStockphoto; pages 16–17, 30–31,
34–35, 48–49, 58–63, 66–73, 76–77, 80–91, 94–95, 100–101, 104–109: © Garrett Olinger; pages 18–19:
© filonmar/iStockphoto; pages 20–21, 96–97, 120–121: © Jorge Salcedo/iStockphoto; pages 22–23:
© Gregory Olsen/iStockphoto; pages 24–25: © David Lentz/iStockphoto; pages 26–27: © manley099/iStockphoto;
pages 28–29: © Anthony Seebaran/iStockphoto; pages 32–33: © ilbusca/iStockphoto; pages 38–39:
© xyno/iStockphoto; pages 40–41: © Marcel Pelletier/iStockphoto; pages 42–43: © Mallory Grigg; pages 44–45:
© Milos Jokic/iStockphoto; pages 46–47: © tomprout/iStockphoto; pages 50–51: © Carsten Brandt/iStockphoto;
pages 52–53: © Nan Moore/iStockphoto; pages 54–55: © Jimmy Anderson/iStockphoto; pages 56–57:
© kickers/iStockphoto; pages 64–65: © Jason Lugo/iStockphoto; pages 74–75: © Sylvie Bouchard/iStockphoto;
pages 78–79: © aurumarcus/iStockphoto; pages 92–93: © traveler1116/iStockphoto; pages 102–103:
© Nicole Hofmann/iStockphoto; pages 110–111: © Gijs Bekenkamp/iStockphoto; pages 112–113:
© Nikada/iStockphoto; pages 114–115: © Claude Beaubien/iStockphoto; pages 116–117: © Kutay Tanir/iStockphoto;
pages 122–123: © Robert E. Schafer/iStockphoto; pages 124–125: © Alistair Scott/iStockphoto; pages 126–127:
© Jeff Giniewicz/iStockphoto; page 128: © Kurt Hahn/iStockphoto.

Published by Price Stern Sloan, a division of Penguin Young Readers Group, 345 Hudson Street, New York,
New York 10014. *PSS!* is a registered trademark of Penguin Group (USA) Inc. Manufactured in Singapore.

ISBN 978-0-8431-6707-8                                                                 10 9 8 7 6 5 4 3 2 1

ALWAYS LEARNING                                                                              **PEARSON**

# TAG THIS!

## THERE ARE NO RULES IN THIS BOOK— NO DIRECTIONS, EITHER!

Do you ever get the urge to scrawl your name across the bathroom wall—in giant letters and permanent marker? Are you powerless to stop yourself from doodling on your schoolbooks, your sneakers, and your younger brother?

Then this is ~~YOUR~~ book! **Chris' BOOK**

There are more than one hundred pages of color photos: toilet stalls, blank walls, gym lockers, billboards, skateboards, cool cars, you name it, all just waiting to be defaced—er, *personalized*.

You can't get in trouble for letting your inner artist run wild here. So grab some markers and start tagging!

PARK

SPACE
AVAILABLE

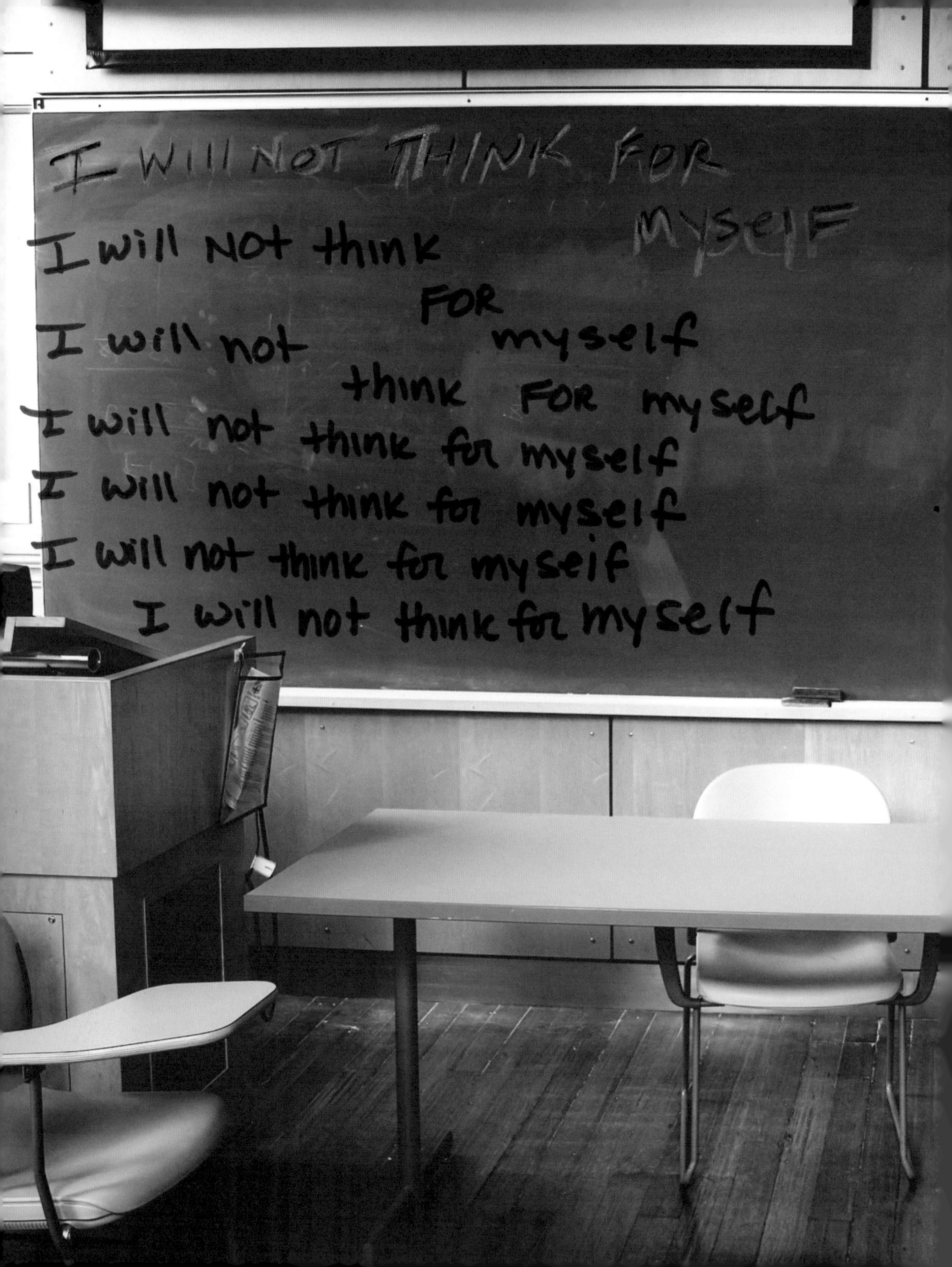

I WILL NOT THINK FOR MYSELF
I will NOT think FOR myself
I will not think FOR myself
I will not think for myself
I will not think for myself
I will not think for myself
I will not think for myself

I will not speak my mind
I will not speak my mind
I will not speak my mind
I will not speak my mind
I will not speak my mind
I will not speak my mind
I will not speak my mind
I will not speak my mind.
I will not speak my mind

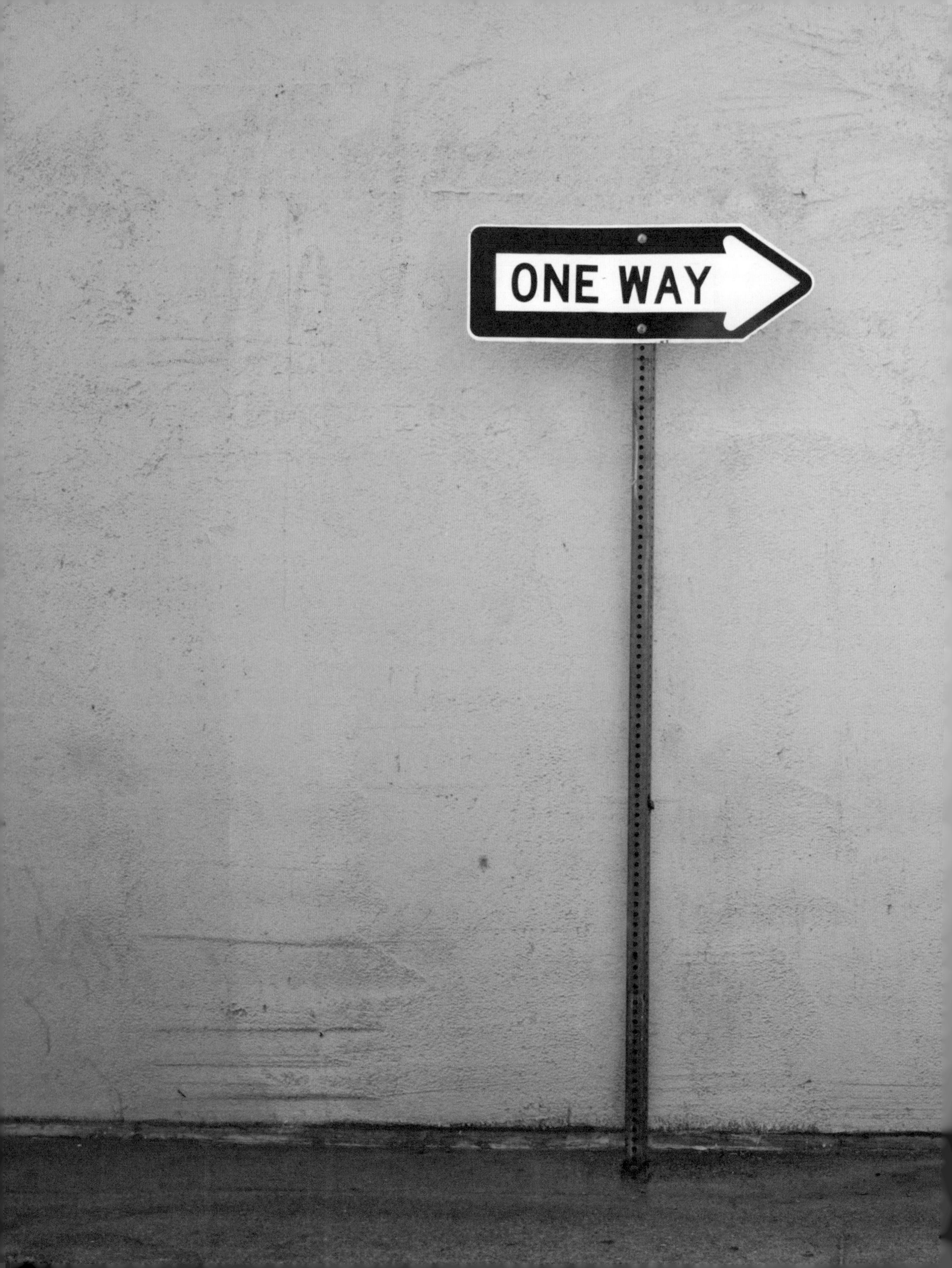
ONE WAY

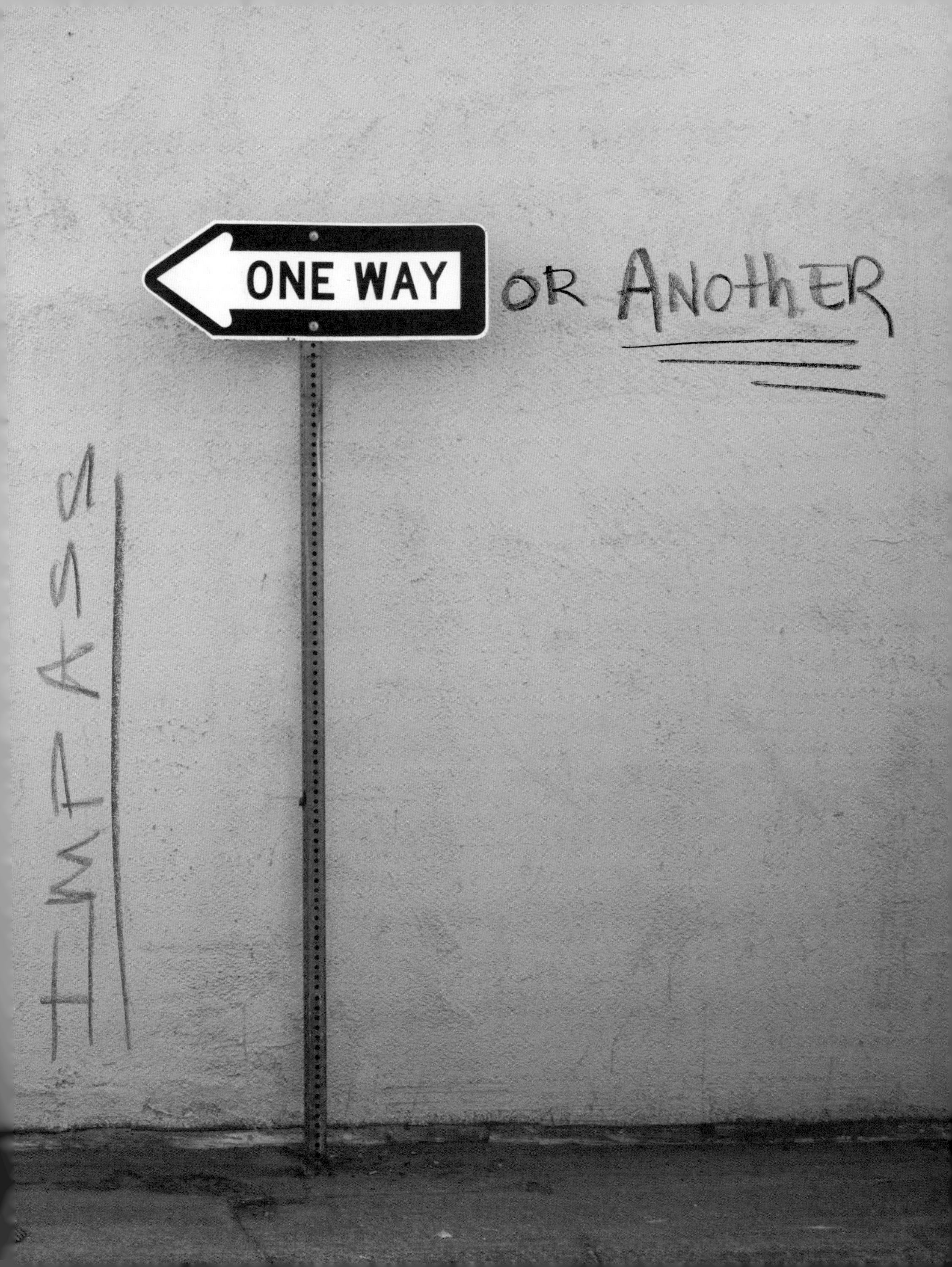
ONE WAY
OR ANOTHER
IMPASS

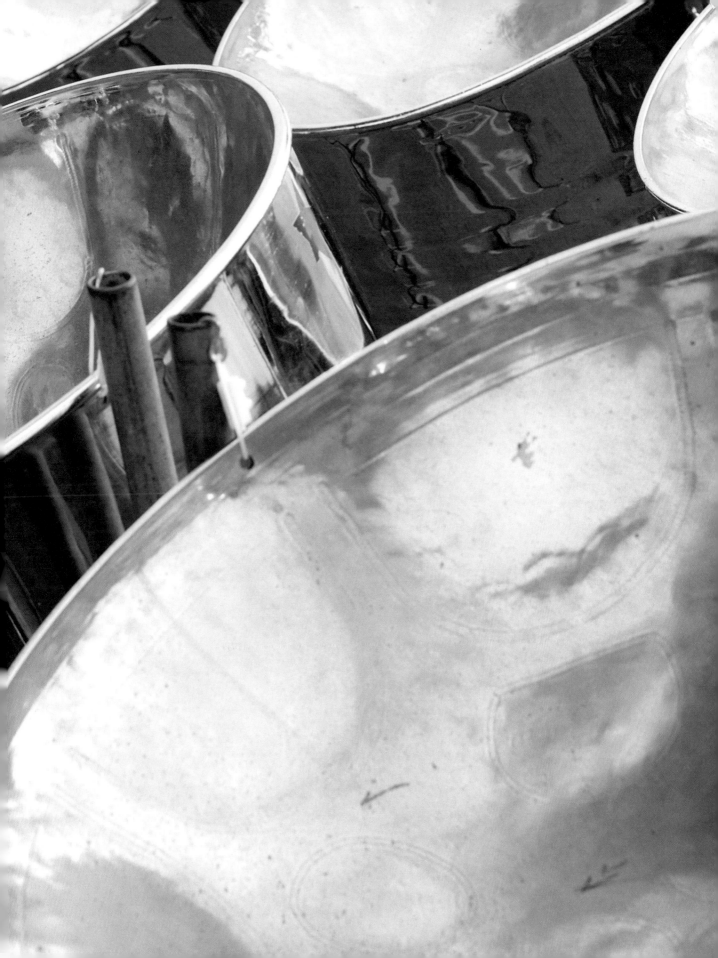

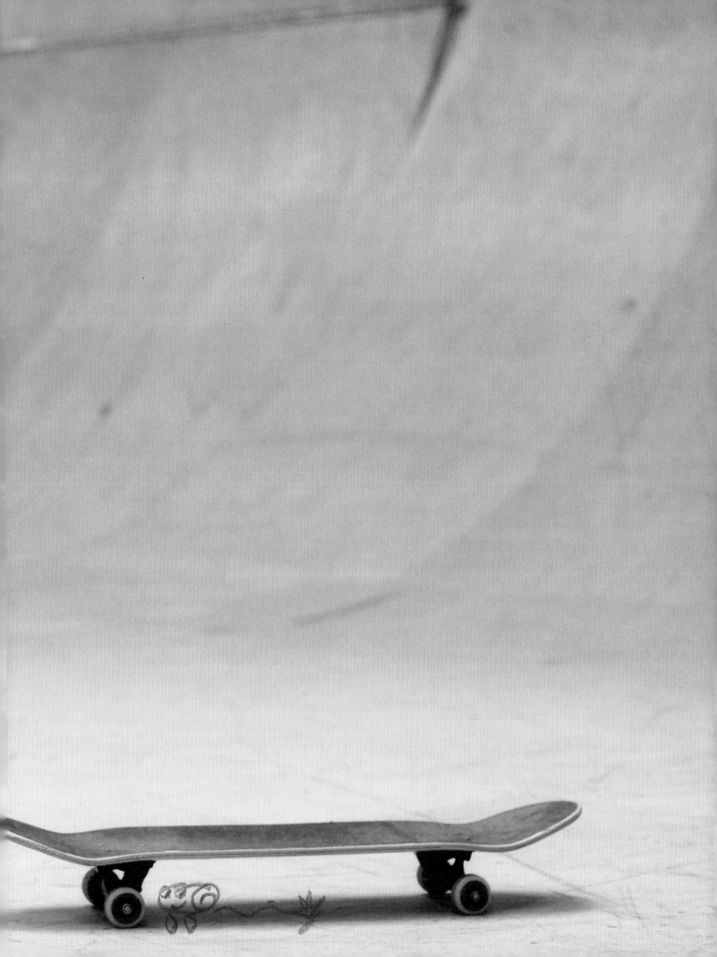

Just because you're Paranoid doesn't mean they Aren't AFTER you!

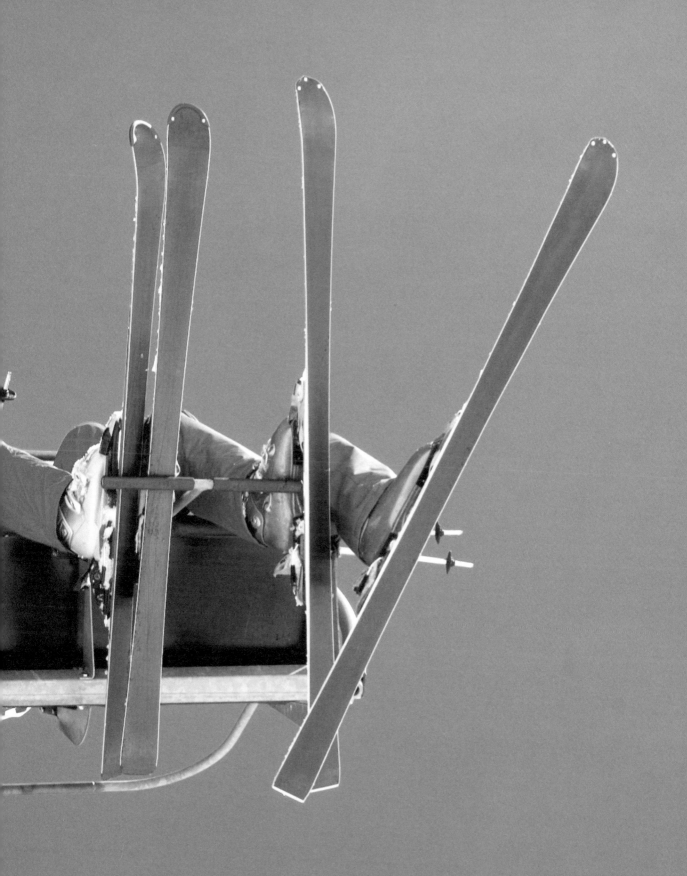